ωιι

ASLEEP AND AWAKE

Poetry

Fairground Music
The Tree That Walked
Cannibals and Missionaries
Epistles to Several Persons
The Mountain in the Sea
Lies and Secrets
The Illusionists
Waiting for the Music
The Beautiful Inventions
Selected Poems 1954 to 1982
Partingtime Hall
(with James Fenton)
The Grey Among the Green
The Mechanical Body
Stones and Fires
Collected Poems
Now and for a Time
Ghosts
The Space of Joy
Song & Dance
Pebble & I
Writing the Picture
(with David Hurn)
Dream Hunter
(with Nicola LeFanu)
New Selected Poems 1983–2008
The Dice Cup
Gravel in My Shoe
AWOL (with Andrew
Wynn Owen)
The Bone Flowers
Double Dactyls

Fiction

Flying to Nowhere
The Adventures of Speedfall
Tell It Me Again
The Burning Boys
Look Twice
The Worm and the Star
A Skin Diary
The Memoirs of Laetitia Horsepole
Flawed Angel
The Clock in the Forest

Criticism

The Sonnet
W. H. Auden: a Commentary
Who is Ozymandias? And Other
Puzzles in Poetry

For Children

Herod Do Your Worst
Squeaking Crust
The Spider Monkey Uncle King
The Last Bid
The Extraordinary Wool Mill and
Other Stories
Come Aboard and Sail Away
You're Having Me On!

As Editor

The Chatto Book of Love Poetry
The Dramatic Works of John Gay
The Oxford Book of Sonnets
W. H. Auden: Poems Selected
by John Fuller
Alexander Pope: Poems Selected
by John Fuller

821 FUL

ASLEEP AND AWAKE

John Fuller

Chatto & Windus
LONDON

1 3 5 7 9 10 8 6 4 2

Chatto & Windus, an imprint of Vintage,
20 Vauxhall Bridge Road,
London SW1V 2SA

Chatto & Windus is part of the Penguin Random House group of companies
whose addresses can be found at global.penguinrandomhouse.com

Copyright © John Fuller 2020

John Fuller has asserted his right to be identified as the author of this Work in
accordance with the Copyright, Designs and Patents Act 1988

First published in the UK by Chatto & Windus in 2020

penguin.co.uk/vintage

A CIP catalogue record for this book is available from the British Library

ISBN 9781784743659

Typeset in 11.75/14pt Dante MT Std by Jouve (UK), Milton Keynes
Printed and bound in Great Britain by Clays Ltd, Elcograf S.p.A.

Penguin Random House is committed to a sustainable future
for our business, our readers and our planet. This book is made
from Forest Stewardship Council® certified paper.

'We wake only briefly into life' —Æsotes of Nisiros

'I was dreaming I was awake, but woke up and
found myself asleep' —Stan Laurel

Contents

Awake and Asleep

Awake and asleep, asleep and awake,
This rhythm rocks me through the night
In dreams, and in the absence of dreams.

'Awake' can take a mark of exclamation
To become a command. Not so 'asleep.'
That state is quite involuntary.

I see it as a metaphor
For falling into my own disuse,
A permanence that is a puzzle

That no one ever gets their head round
Since the discovery that God
Has forgotten to cry 'Sleep no more!'

To have ever become awake at all
Seems a great privilege, and something
Of an accident, all things considered.

It's an enchantment like a spell
Still unbroken, never postponed,
As sleep is, for present pleasures.

Waking is what we daily hope for.
Oblivion is a total forgetting
Of everything that has occurred.

And out of this rhythm arrives a sudden
Play of mind, not only the dream
With its obscure contrivances

But the thought that becomes a kind of key
To the lock that dreaming fumbles at,
The truth, the memory, the poem.

In War Time

1. Talking to myself in 1942

(On my poppy, filling my pipe
With tufts of chocolate packing-straw
From Bernie's oilskin pouch, poking
It down with Granny's chicken skewer).

Well now, let's see. (Suck, suck, suck).
This skewer is precious. Skewers are scarce
Because hens are scarce, you know (suck, suck).
I'm just going to read to my little Jezza.

Please don't be impatient. Oh, poor
Henrietta, but she shouldn't have gone
Over the giant's hill. Where is my
Father Christmas pencil-sharpener?

(The cut-out cardboard theatre
Lit by a flickering candle-stub
Glimmers with the colours of treasure
And the almond smell of glue).

That's Aladdin. Are those boys
Laddins too? Where is Johnny?
You'd better go and find him.
I'm underneath the table!

Will I have five candles on my cake?
What happens when I get to 100?
And who will make my cake?
Because you'll be dead then.

2. Grandfather Clock

A door in the clock: someone
Needs to go in and out.
But no one ever sees him.
He sees everyone,
Like a spy with a briefcase.

It thuds and knocks
Like an endless headache.
The sound is transmitted
As a secret signal
From the nether world.

Each reluctant tick
Just slightly louder than
The last, or less loud,
Successfully defying
Regularity.

It is a house with no floors
And no stairs, only
A carven darkness
With ratchets and pulleys,
A coffin for time.

It is a vain pretence
For making peace with
The sleeping household,
Saying: dead-dead-
Dead-dead-dead.

3. Granny's Chicken Soup

A week of fever, eating nothing,
Unable to glance at Tiger Tim.
I haul myself weakly up the pillows
To find a tray upon my knees.

I do not know that I might have died,
Never waking one morning and not
Knowing that I had not woken,
And no one tells me at the time.

The soup bowl is an opened planet
Of slowly revolving essences,
A small ocean whose warm rim
Reminds me how cool I feel now.

I touch the level of the clear broth
Delicately beaded with fat,
A bright suspension which the spoon
Dispels to the circumference.

I dip further down to the depths
To stir the hidden store of fibrous
Finely-chopped bits of breast,
Strangely dry in their savoury juices.

And I am Tim in full colour,
The leader of the Bruin Boys.
Taste becomes a jolly adventure
Of newsprint exclamation marks.

Somewhere else the war goes on
With its dispersal and collapse,
Its hospital beds like wrapped farm gates
And heroic chums in black-and-white.

4. *Awake*

After the many terrors of the night,
When darkness is complete and no one comes,
The window slowly pales, making the shape of light.

Breakfast is the hour celebrating its sounds:
Creak of the stairs and raking of the coals,
The milkman's yodel, and the clop of his horse.

5. Ground Rice Moulds

How nice, how very nice!
Just a little rice:
Lost in the liquid,
It seethes to thicken.

The old tin moulds
Themselves seem cold:
Utilitarian
Armour in the larder.

In batches like bullets
Three-quarters full,
Sides slightly dented
Like silver fezzes.

Turn out the mould
Of grainy vanilla
And pour on the syrup,
The white and the gold!

6. *Ice-cream*

A tuppenny one from Mrs Foster
Who churned it in her yard,
Stout in her corsets
And a Chinese peignoir.

Or a wafer from Pablo's
Like a mortared brick
Licked at the melting edges,
Leaving white smudges.

Where does the cold come from
All the summer long?
The roof of the mouth
Is numb to the tongue.

7. Grandpa's Car

The leather cracked and anointed,
The Bakelite and chrome
Dutifully maintained,
It preserves a strange power,
Sitting in its dark palace
Like a dispossessed monarch.

Petrol is known to be precious,
And finely calculated.
A fowl without points
Is worth the journey,
Green garage doors scraped back
For the farm in the Fylde.

That nonchalance, the rim
Of the steering wheel between
The third and fourth finger,
One elbow at rest upon
The lowered window, lips
Pursed in a silent whistle.

8. War Effort

Spills to light fires,
Yellow, purple, green,
Plaited into mats
Making roofs and walls
For a busy lead farmyard.

Turkeys on the carpet
Always falling over.
The cow resting like a sofa.
A girl with yoked pails
Who will never pour them out.

This is our life going on
In front of the shifting coals
And their rosy light reflected
In the shovel, the delicate tongs,
And the dimpled brass of the scuttle,

What hero is awaited
With mustard-coloured Stetson
And one loosely hinged arm
Who will give his broad grin
And direct operations?

It's a lonely game, a simple
Trial of arrangements
Where an established story
Is gradually displaced
Into a possible tomorrow

When the pilots return
To the fields their burning planes
Spiralled above, and the past
Will only exist for us
In their unreadable faces.

9. Grandpa Asleep

I'm on the hillside of a waistcoat,
Not struggling to be free but like a cat
Tense to that possibility
Should it wonderfully occur.

Is he pretending to be asleep?
Am I pretending not to mind?
How did I get here on to his lap?
Did I ever finish my tea?

Toying with his thin grey hair,
Feeling the growling of his digestion,
Intermittent like a biplane
Trailing advertisements above the sand.

If free, I might be running there,
Keeping up with its moving shadow
Or pursued by it like a condor,
My feet slowed down in the brown sugar.

As it is, Grandpa's not moving.
The clock ticks ever so slowly
And seems to be smothering the minutes.
That's why it's called a Grandfather Clock.

Sometime soon Granny will come in
And tell him: 'Harry, get the coal in!'
But just for now the hillside moves
Up and down, in time with his snores.

10. Horses at Newmarket

Of that quartet, a dog-eared paste-board stable,
The least considered is the Ace of Spades
Standing like an inverted stabbed black heart,
A pedestal upon a gleaming table.
Grandpa's favourite is the 'Jack-of-Hearts!'
Showing a fist above his patched brocades,
Vermilion and green, with frieze of yellow,
Wearing a narrow, sprung mustachio,
So luscious, yet somehow a pained fellow.
And his royal cousin, the King of Diamonds,
One palm in prayer or appeal, the ends
Of his combed hair and full beard lightly curled,
A halberd at his back, ruling a world
Shared with the neat red royals, but mostly his.
And yet these are as nothing to my eyes
Compared with the Queen of Clubs, stiff-caped and sour,
Her blood the swart of clustered blackberries,
A dazzling bodice, and in her hand a flower.

The Ace is easily and early played
And not much backed, as might befit a spade
That boldly tells the singleness of graves.
The Jack is preciously a Knave of Knaves:
Though freely backed, he comes a frequent cropper.
The ruby King, whose powers are absolute,
Joins him in blood and riskiness of playing,
Though when once played he is a certain stopper.
It is the Queen, the conscience of her suit
Who is the sleekest, chanciest horse for me,

Backed against all the odds, though left behind.
With bets held over, her singleness of mind
And thunderous frown speak of finality.
At the next round, then, corner to corner, edge
By edge, forming the kitty, I am weighing
My chances with the horses. Though it seems vain
She might turn up, my eager privilege
Is putting my ha'penny on the Queen again.

11. Grandpa's Radio

The oracle has secrets. The dial
Draws its needle in a yellow window
Through many urgent stations,
Heard and unheard in an instant
Like voices in a river.

His fingers turn, though to pause
Is to focus, not to choose,
And should not stray
Beyond the glow of Hilversum
And unnerving Babel.

The voice of authority
Emerges with familiar clarity.
Who knew the world of war
To be so distant, so busy
And so small?

12. Facing Either Way

There, behind glass in the front room,
A saucy doll of matte ceramic
With a fabric skirt and knitted cap
That swivels forward over her face

Revealing at her occiput
A second, darker face, turning
The posture of her offered kiss
Into an inching, guarded retreat.

I would be happy to kiss either.
My king is still the Emperor of India
And I his subject like all the others
Scattered across the throbbing globe.

13. Granny in the Bath

I want to play with it again,
Grandpa's weighted precision razor,
The thick-based blade lolloping backwards
And forwards, tugged on its leather strop.

So I wander into the bathroom
Where Granny is surprisingly having a bath.
'Don't look!' she says, uncertain whether
The simply accidental is ever forbidden.

I know that a full bath imagines
The shapes of everyone who uses it,
All the different islands and displacements
Produced by its concealing depth.

I know that its use creates steam
Clouding the tiles and the trickling mirror
Which you can then rub off with your hand
In an instant picture of your own face.

My cheeks are burning and I stare out of the window.
I lift the strop for a calculated moment,
My head dizzy with disbelief in knees
And the separation of the bosom.

And I hear and imagine all the noises
Of this, the most private room in the house,
The laboratory of the cherished body:
The tap dripping into the unstirred surface.

The desperate gulping of the water tank.
The weeping of the lavatory. And I do not wait
For the slurping of the twisted plughole
Like a straw chasing the last lemonade.

14. Talking to myself in 1944

Since the German war broke out
Two bombers have reached Africa.
Our allies (long pause)
Are putting up a glorious fight.

Men like news. (Granny
Likes Mint Imperials,
Tiny pebble eggs in their offered
Nest of crumpled paper).

Why is there no sea in London?
Now look, I don't want any more
No damned nonsense. I think
This war will go on for ever, don't you?

(The newsreel unfolds like a flag
And is folded up again.
Sweet music is an enchantment
That lights up the coughing darkness.

For a time, Stan and Ollie
Are wearing each other's bowler hats.
Now look what you've gone
And made me do! Give it here!

The dwarfs crowd the banister
And rush down to their soup.
Beneath the table, I can touch
The decorations on their clogs).

15. Asleep

The man in the clock waits
Until it is dark, and then I know
That I will find it hard to get past him
Through the corners and the shadows.

I am tucked up in the attic.
And not meant to be awake,
But although I am drowsy
I am too anxious to be asleep.

I could launch myself from the door-frame.
Crouching, I could slowly
Leap down all the diagonals
Without the stairs creaking.

I try to catch myself at the moment
Of not being awake, the moment
When I know that I am asleep,
So that I can prevent it.

16. Treasure in the Attic

Gleaming trays framed in walnut
With thread conduits, secret routes
Through tiny hooks and shuttles.

Slit slabs of polished steel
With sinuous motion that drew in
Needles and ejected them.

Eyelet makers, surgery
Of cuffs, shirt-fronts and lapels,
Profuse wincing of invisible stitching.

Miniature machined extras
That somehow don't fit together,
Parts of a mysterious whole

Which once whirred round and round,
Brilliant as the glances of seraphs
Pile-driven through our lazy thumbs.

17. Remember, Remember

Remember David Thompson, whose fingers had been snapped off
    when his father slammed the car door;
    And the smell of the leather seats in the sun;

Remember Wendy Yates's trophy box of decorations: owl-pipe, cones
    and oak-apples;
    And the lower-case 'i' for Indian-with-a-feather and 'r' for
    rose-in-a-vase;

Remember Barbara Bennett making crusty flour pies beneath the
    kitchen table;
    And the mad woman who scooped phlegm from the pavement and
    ate it;

Remember John Harcourt sharing twizzers and Cherry-go-rips;
    And the crayon drawing of Joe Carioca;

Remember Ann Clarkson with her red hair and faded greeny frock;
    And the amazement at her joined-up writing;

Remember Robin Aird, whose mother brought home-made lemonade
    across the long lawn;
    And the ha'penny fare on the bus;

Remember Cousin Sheila, who got most of the kitties in Newmarket;
    And what we found in the monks' bench;

Remember Brian Baxter, who told me that if they ever removed the
    rubber thing from his groin he would die;
    And the 84 red badges of chicken-pox;

Remember Michael O'Connor staying on for cod and ice-cream;
    And *Look Out!* By E. Sawyer Cumming;

Remember being at long last eight years old, knowing few but these
    early random fruits of my frail human kin;

Remember, remember, and the thudding orchard.

Only Child

I was the first child and the second, too,
Questioning my mother about her intentions
Until she realised I'd bear no rival
Unless it was myself. I was already jealous
Of those who were never to come after me.
I had the first child's inquisitive slyness
And the second child's rage for a share of attention.
I was both overpraised for my modest talents
And neglected enough to develop them all by myself.
I was both lonely and introspective, and confident and
    cheeky.
I teased and protected myself like a brother,
And both obeyed and rebelled against the family
    conventions.
This is the strange double life of the only child,
Nursing an absence that will never go away.

Fulehung

for Daniel

The Fulehung like a lunatic
With a bouncing bladder on a stick
Runs through the streets of Thun.
Its mask is horned, its mouth a slit,
Half-terror, half-buffoon.
There is no stopping it.

The memory of where I stood
In those deserted streets
Beneath an icy demilune
Comes back to me, for though
I ran as hard as ever I could,
I did not stir a foot.

The Fulehung will find me
In the silent shadowed square.
The Fulehung will find me
Although I am not there.
The Fulehung is behind me,
Its nose a bulb of blood.

The face that groans in the stomach,
The eyes that ache like a cave,
The mask that stares from the mirror,
The lips that never forgave
Are all that define the Fulehung,
Who's there to make me behave.

Down my back the discs were strung,
Into my arms the hinges put,
My legs locked in their sockets:
I cannot run for ever through my life
With bones that cry out to the skies
And nothing in my pockets.

I'd licked the ink to play the fool
And legends stained my tongue.
I waited in the midnight room
With its clump of fallen soot
And silent stood the Fulehung.
Silent stood the ghoul.

I cannot run, and yet I run
More than I ever did
When half in terror, half in play,
Panting, I stopped and hid.
Now in the gradual dwindling of the day
I run, but cannot run.

The Fulehung has found me
With its bladder and its grin
In the lava-flow of my desires,
Where standing pools and turgid fires
And silence's ecstatic din
Are all around me.

My ribs are like a ladder
On which my heart took fright.
I look upon my life in fear,
As if from unaccustomed height
Where everything at last is clear:
The Fulehung has found me.

Trawling

So fine a net, we thought
    It could not fail.
All night—uncertainty!
    Trawling for revelation
    With lowered sail,
And the long skeins unfolding
    Into the sea.

Our quest—more than a question
    Idly asked and answered,
More than appraisal of the best
    That makes the best what it is,
    And more than mere chance:
Again and again we hurl our nets,
And over the oily waves
    The lanterns dance.

There is an art in judging
    The fineness of a mesh
    That sweeps and winnows.
We think the weave is coarse enough
    To leave the waste behind:
It is like the still ponds of our youth
Where we sat all day in the sun
    And what did we find?
We hoped for narwhals and mermaids
    And brought up minnows.

The Pact

Summer is suddenly upon us, as the sun
Wastes itself freely, and small purposes with wings
And legs make busy noises in the bushes.
But you, you find yourself just at a moment
Of vague self-questioning and emptiness
When to remember all the yous that you have been
Is as unlikely as knowing who you might be next.

It feels like the successful adoption of masks at a party,
Where the one person who knows you all too well
Has, all this time, been hovering at your elbow,
And before he can say a word, you vainly pre-empt him:
'Don't think me ungrateful,' you say to this old friend.
'I can't fault you. You made it all perfectly clear
Right from the start, or at least when it made most sense.'

And what is it that you pretend to find so hard?
Is it something that the bee demonstrates?
Being one thing? Simple and purposeful?
You have often remade this pact with your inquisitor
Who gave you your choice in the first place, the one that in truth
You acknowledge at every moment: 'Give me the skill
To face my death, and I will freely live first.'

In Whose Head?

Schumann, op. 41, no. 2.

When at last in old age I listen again
To the music of my youth, it finally speaks
Nothing to me of my father, who shared it with me
(That lilt in the second movement, for example, something
Like a folk-song, almost a fore-echo of Richard Strauss).
It is familiar to me only as itself, nothing else.
I am inside the head of its begetter, not my own,
And yet its sound over the years, hasn't it changed?
Not just the somewhat unlikely tempo of these players,
But the whole charge and depth of its lucid argument?
Surely it has, for why now would it make me weep?

Thrush

This bird, rejoicing in
His five notes, one by one,
Doesn't decide to begin
But seems to have just begun.

'Come again to me!'
Down, up, up, down again,
Blossom on the tree,
Blossom in the rain.

'Come again to me!
Dewy, dewy, dew!'
Repeated ecstasy,
Which is forever new.

How does he manage this
Sublime response to the day's
Paling, the artifice
Of his shrill five-note phrase?

Dawn's transformation
To sounds that pierce and climb,
A moment's inspiration
Repeated for all time.

Light of the stirring earth,
Breath in a liquid shout
Of all that life is worth,
Of what life is about.

'Come again to me!
Jenny, Jenny, Jenny!'
The notes precise but free,
And not a note too many.

Butterflies

for Adam and Jo

Beginning in Wales in a fine Mehefin
With cabbage whites among the nettles;
Then the one that bothered Đjoković
As he crouched behind the useless net;
Continuing in Devon, that black pair
Circling on their invisible bolas
Over the parched lawns of the Hall;
And then in Coumbelous the fluttering cloud
Of tiny blues beside the pool
As the world drifted into August;
The distracted prisoners at Micropolis;
And another flashing its rose-window
Above the khaki Salendrenque
Where the libellules conducted something
Like a military evacuation;
And the shyer one lurching across
The baking terrace at St Clair.
It is the high summer of the butterflies,
And we have shared it with them.

Being and Time

Thrown into being, we feel nothing at all,
Not a loss, and certainly not a fall.
And if not a loss, then there is nothing to lose.
On the contrary, there is everything to choose.

And yet we somehow resent having to choose.
We don't want this or that. We want it all.
We want to succeed. We've no desire to lose.
So we extemporize. All summer and fall,

Winter and spring, the torturing seasons fall
Into place, their beauty compelling us to choose
Each crucial turning, so that we do not lose
Our way. There simply is no time, that's all.

What will befall us? It's time that makes us choose,
And at the end of time we lose it all.

Warnings

These small warnings are trivial in themselves,
Like the clues in a mystery that will explain everything.
They gradually form into a pattern of significant decline
To tell you that your mother has at last finished with you.
She shaped you as carefully as she could
With all that she had, and sent you out
To your long play in those once endless days.

But now the lizard skin, the knotting of veins,
The lumbar drag, the ache in the shoulders,
The poached eyes, the thudding behind the ears,
The unbending joints, the diminished senses:
Which of these heralds the final exasperated shout
That will bring you in at last, at bedtime,
Tired out, yes, but reluctant as always?

Paralysis

Only the unapproachable emperor could say
Where the battle raged, or if it raged at all.

His limitless campaigns were done. On either
Hand the generals retired in shame.

Orders returned riderless, the colours collapsed.
There was no forward movement, no movement back.

Mind turned in vain to the dim and printed
Geography of his remembered empire.

Panic is nothing but the staring eye
Of a single candle wildly burning in his tent.

Fathers

Such tender-hearted dandies,
Kicking in tight-groined trousers
Of ostentatious stripe
Upon a soupy pond!

Through clustered cresses
They edge forwards or sideways
To guard the cloudy masses
Of their waking progeny.

They are spruce acrobats
As much as patient fathers,
Somehow aware of our presence
But not of our sense of pathos.

The day will come soon
When those dribs and commas
Will be ready to wriggle away.
Will they all be eaten?

Or will the pond dry up?
The fathers know nothing of either.
They do not hope or pray.
They have no memories.

But their spread hands make peace
With unknown enemies
Over the still waters,
And keep their balance.

The Giant

for Sophie and Elaine

Can you see the giant at the end of the street?
Between those balconied façades? You lift
Your head up: where the dwindling roof tops meet
The sky, he's there, slumbering and somnolent.
He's guarding his generous but unwanted gift,
The hoard of fire that is his secret excitement.
The entire city is paved with his hot black tears.
His single eye is a weeping crust. He fears
That he's unloved. He's utterly bored all day,
Scowling at his irritating rival the sun.
His long fingers stir the steaming bay.
We glance warily at him now and then,
And somewhat admiringly, for his very presence,
His unbelievable size, and his great forbearance.

Mistral

Maestro, this conduct is unbecoming:
Fury without purpose, neither frustration
Nor appetite. The waves fall like pianist's fingers
In thunderous octaves on the foaming beach
    And never quite reach
      A resolution.

Yours is a purely abstract passion,
A marriage of different temperaments,
A surge in the attention of distant air
That pretends to know what it is doing
    (Burly Biscay wooing
      The ennui of Genoa).

It leaves us in the position of onlookers
Distracted by righteous quarrels, buffeted
By mere emptiness, by displacement,
By being continually assaulted and pinned
    Down by an idiot wind,
      Unchanged by it.

Tornado

Across the entire map of our ordered life
   The dark finger lifts. It leaves nothing
      To our imagination, and at last
         It is defiantly and nakedly revealed
            As something simple, a force of nature.
               But strangely we cannot quite see it.
            It is there as a tower of cloud
         Across the squared plain like a chess piece.
      Lifting cows and houses, it turns, stubborn and wilful,
   And lofts the splinters it has finished with.
How it stamps on all the fences!
   Everyone in hiding. No one to see
      The damage surrounding the centre.
         That buzzing stillness is defined by
      The damage surrounding the centre.
   Everyone in hiding. No one to see
How it stamps on all the fences
   And lofts the splinters it has finished with,
      Lifting cows and houses. It turns stubborn and wilful
         Across the squared plain like a chess piece.
         It is there as a tower of cloud,
            But strangely we cannot quite see it
         As something simple, a force of nature.
         It is defiantly and nakedly revealed
      To our imagination. And at last
   The dark finger lifts. It leaves nothing
Across the entire map of our ordered life.

Siege

for Nicola LeFanu

1. Vigil

The baby wakes.
The baby wakes in the hour of the morning
When the air is cool as silk
And the pale bird of the night gives way
To the crimson bird of the day.
The baby wakes, his fingers at my milk.

I feel the feeling of his fingers,
The tremor at the end of his hands
When he grasps me at the dawning of the day.
He takes his fill, and sleeps again,
But his mouth lingers, taking its sips,
And the tongue still moves a little against his lips.

This is our land, which we work with our hands.
This is our land, where we have put down a root.
This is our land, and our hands know it
As our hands once knew our mothers.
The land is rich in its honey and milk
And its prodigious memory of fruit.

The land is a gift, a divine covenant,
Twice given, twice blest,
But given in guilt, given in shame,
A hope renewed, day after day
As the baby is made in equal love and pain.
The hands that give can also take away.
The land that is given is also taken away.

2. Terror

Son of my body, you go from me.
Your hand that slipped from my breast,
Your hand that slipped from mine, ready for pleasure,
Your hand that slipped from mine, ready for trouble,
Your hand that worked the land,
Has been put to different work,
The work of joy, and the work of pain,
For the land that is given is given in guilt
And the land is taken that we have built.

When they told me who to hate, I did not believe them.
But if your enemy is destroyed, how can you grieve?
I thought my enemy had a human face.
I could look and see myself in that dark place
Where only hatred breeds in the land
And the hand that is ready for trouble
Does everything that may be done by a hand.

The hand that held the breast will pluck the fruit.
The hand that plucked the fruit will tighten on the gun.
For the fruit of the land is the fruit of exile
And the fruit of guilt is the pulling up of the root
That binds all people to an unforgiving land
And the pulling of the trigger is the fruit of hatred.

The baby wakes.
The baby wakes in the hour of the morning
When the air is full of heat and dust
And the peace of the night gives way

To the crimson beast of the day.
The apartments are sliced open like a doll's house,
The families in dust, as stiff as dolls,
Children in rubble, unusually still.
In the hospitals, the surgeons in despair,
The beds themselves under rubble,
A thigh stump like a burst pomegranate.

The baby wakes in his mother's blood,
Reaching into indistinguishable space
Where the dying are darkened and whimpering
Like dogs who have been shut out of their lives.

3. Lament

This is our country.
This is our covenant.
This is our citadel.
This is our pride.
This is our government.
This is our shame,
When death is the work of hands:
This one a murderer.
This one a hero.
This is the enemy I have defiled.
This is an act in defence of our land.
This is an act committed by a child.

This is a human face
That could be the face of anyone
Staring from a mirror
When guilt is discovered
Like the signs of an illness,

Like an unforeseeable error,
Something that was once begun
In all good will, and must be endured.
This is what our children have done.
This is the quietness before the terror.
This is the explosion before the stillness.
This is the warning, and the gun.

. . .

We lobbed into the citadel
Gifts that unwrapped themselves in smoke,
With bursts of fire like whirling threads.

Our mortars lifted sounds from hell
To deafen the whole air and spell
In dust the sentences they spoke.

And all day long the houses broke.
The daughters bled into their beds.
Night was on fire, and when we woke

Death was all round us with its smell,
The fathers silent where they fell,
The mothers wailing from their heads.

And every pain was ours as well,
Our children's pain. How can it be
That a child is someone's enemy?

Were we outside the citadel?
Were we inside the citadel?
It seemed the same. No one could tell.

4. Prayer

This is my child, who will never wake,
Patrolling the streets with a ready gun,
Waiting with explosives in a tunnel,
Doing what is done with human hands,
The fruit spilling from the market carts.

Now he is asleep in the hour of the morning
When the air has the bitter smell of death
And the pale bird of the night gives way
To the black bird of the day,
To the heaviness of limbs and the stifling of breath.

Now he is dead, and heavy in my arms.
I feel the weight of him in my arms,
And not a breath escapes his lips.
Where can we go? What can we do?
The walls are burning, and the locked ships.

There is no end to a siege when both sides are besieged.
There is no end to the suffering of each.
There is no end to this, no end
Until the enemy becomes a friend,
And the fruit again grows freely in the field.

So here I pray for the need to be revealed,
And the will to answer to the need,
When the voice of mothers will be believed
When the night will in the end give way
To the perfect reason of the day.

Allâhumma allif bayna qulûbinâwa aslih dhâta
baynina wahdinâ subûl as-salam.

Oseh shalom bim'romav
Hu ya'aseh shalom aleynu
V'al kol Yisrael
V'imru Amen.

Stationary

for Sophie

Brisk through the barrier
Come the commuters
Hastening home.

The platform propels
Them, those who pause
To trash *The Times*

And those crossing the concourse,
Heads held high,
At a clip for the car park.

Or those relative
Tyros of travel
With tendered tickets

Asking the advice
Of the aimless attendants
And stopping to stare.

Tourists in twos
With matching mufflers
And great grins.

The drained day-shopper
Spotting her spouse
With a sudden smile.

The doyen of the dinner
Already in DJ
And patting his speech.

I stand in stillness,
Single and stationary
Among the multitude.

As always with waiting,
The one that I wish for
Is nearly the last.

Others I thought
I might have been meeting
Are a strange distraction.

The half-known faces,
The famous philosopher
Laughing to himself.

The girl with the gun
(Or a fencing foil?)
Slung over her shoulder.

The neighbour needing
Something of a signal,
Or a local lift.

A procession like pages
Of a futile fiction,
Till, suddenly dazzling,

That familiar face
With expectant eyes
Moving to mine.

Cool-cheeked and cherished
In a broad embrace.
Perfect. Expected.

Te Ika-a-Māui

for Joe

You've come to the fabled coast
Of Coromandel, where
The gods once fished for islands
And now the fish play there.

We think of you descending
To Lonely Bay, where you trudge
Through the granular dissolution
Of rock, the sea's long grudge.

The tide speaks its old language
Of horizon and adventure,
The lure of the seven-tenths
To some distant event.

You are bound in your own body
Like a young fish in a net,
But you wear your bold resolve,
And the appropriate amulet.

What prayers are needed for you?
What concentration of
Concern, hope and outcome
Which triangulates our love?

The gods may be capricious
In their assumption of powers
That trouble us, but that
Is their affair, not ours.

A Week in Bern

for Felix

1. Hotel Goldener Schlüssel

Hotels are comedies of self-possession:
The francs and passports safe in the wardrobe locker,
We go to dinner with a grave discretion,
To the joking waiter and the 'Suure Mocke'
And afterwards stroll at a steady pace
Through the old city (arcade upon arcade
Smelling of vanilla) to find some place
To stop for a *stumpe* and a lemonade.

Our faces carry with them what we're thinking,
And phrases from our books hang in the air,
Cultural baggage that punctuates our drinking.
Pumblechook says: '*May* I . . . ?', pulls up a chair
For Monopoly Deal. We're only half-awake.
Kris Kringle says: 'You're making a mistake!'

2. Fountains

I was last here in the 'eighties, giving a reading
With Somhairle MacGill-Eain (at home among the mountains
With his own mountain language, and I a willing
Tenant of such heights). Dear City of Fountains
With its sixteen grotesque spoutings, arching and spilling
In the long streets beneath their painted myths,
Saints in attitudes of pain or pleading,
Heraldic obelisks and monoliths!

You liked the one we ate beneath at lunch
One day al fresco in the Kornhausplatz:
A giant with babies tucked inside his belt
Appeared to eat them, one by one. We felt
He might have been a rat-catcher with rats,
Except that these were babies. Munch, munch, munch.

3. *Two Rivers*

The shoppers stream before us and are gone:
A fräulein wearing shades like a tiara
And dressed in animal skins; stiff-backed old men
With buttoned collars and check caps and coughs;
A laughing couple eating chocolate;
Eddies of people, while you dodge in and out.
Although we think of you as getting tall,
Your shape at times can hardly be seen at all,
Until you return, make contact with a shout.
You seem to like the thought of getting wet.
You perch on conduits and leap from troughs
As if pure energy were flight. And then
You peel off socks and dip toes in the Aare.
Which takes no notice of you, and flows on.

4. *Strassenschachspiel in the Bundesplatz*

He's the most casual of casual players,
A rook hooked under the fingers, put in place
With a quarter roll, like a barrel, on its base.
His moves appear to take him unawares,
Although he makes them. Down he stares,

A pawn in one hand like a violin case.
He kicks a knight away and makes a face
At it. The pieces rock upon their squares.

The size of this allows for little patience.
With pocket sets you work out combinations
Over and over. Perfection's in your head.
But in the street it's like that living game
Where queens made moves on kings not just in name,
And pieces taken really had to be dead.

5. *Sparrows Chez Edy*

Swiss sparrows, alert and somehow creamier
Than other sparrows, fattened on the crumbs
Of *flammküchen*, eager as academia
To move among the tables like small vacuums
Pouncing on the footnotes of our tarts,
These unctuous texts of ham and emmenthal
Cut like a pizza into several parts,
Once horizontal, five times vertical.

What taste! And what discrimination!
They mime the waiters in their swift attendance
As if to satisfy our every wish,
And though they show a nervous independence
Their little heads are cocked in approbation
To compliment us on our choice of dish.

6. *The Jacquemart on the Zytglogge*

This tower was once a prison for priests' whores.
Now time itself is held a captive here,

With hidden clockwork and mysterious laws
Of circled astrolabe and planisphere,
The coloured zodiac, and little doors
Where peasant shapes appear and disappear.
A bearded Chronos, taking up the cause
Of lost eternity, defends the year.

In armour of the European wars,
With a hinged elbow like a lobster's shell
And stout gold greaves, to much applause
He sweeps his golden hammer at the bell.
Is time his enemy? There is a pause
Before it's struck. Now only time will tell.

7. Gormley at the Zentrum Paul Klee

Signor Piano played his arpeggios
Upon this hill outside the city where
Octaves of glass and girder interpose
Three rolling curves between the grass and air
And trees sprout in the hidden porticoes.

The trams make statements, too, the clang and sway
Of a machine that's always pleased to take
The visitor across the bridge, away
And up to Kirchenfeld, all for art's sake.

And what we find there is a grid-like space
With cuboid hominids—an installation.
Up and down the rigid ranks you race,
Responding to this sudden realisation:
The body is not an object but a place.

8. Klee Revisited

'A childish moonlit scene. A fishing smack.
The cries of yellow birds beside the lake.
The image is disturbing. Something black—
A screaming lidless mask. A hideous mistake.' [1953]

Unheimlich, yes: as though the forest track
You trod was not the one you thought you'd take,
As though you'd found the place through turning back,
As though you dreamed and yet were still awake.
But colour's careful as the zodiac.
Arrows of flight or disapproval make
Jokes of themselves. The pencil has a knack
Of turning sideways just for the pretty sake
Of it. At seventy-seven I have seen
Beyond the melodrama of sixteen. [2014]

9. Marie Stauffer, in the year of her father's death

In any gallery there will be one
Real face that looks at you across the years,
Like this one painted by Karl Stauffer-Bern
Of his sad sister. Her hair is bunched upon
Her head and partly drawn behind her ears
To frame a brow that's lofty like a cairn
Upon a mountain, capping a distant view
Above an eye paired with another eye,
Twin caves of mourning questioning a blue
That seems to claim that nothing will ever die.
They are divided by a nose of sense,
A nose of duty guarding the mouth, wherein
Emotion, grateful for that stout defence,
Is held, like wine, above a trembling chin.

10. Ferdinand Hodler

Loading his brush, he knows what paint must do,
The upraised arm and the attentive eyes
Bring all his body with them, straight out through
The fingers, where the final shaping lies.
So paint explores that taut expressive play
Of skin that is the body's primal vesture:
Mouth that has closed on what it had to say,
Hands that descry in a hieratic gesture
The wonder and bewilderment of sex,
Or clutch the sheets in terror of the night.
It's paint that lifts the trousered woodman's axe
To the canvas's far corner. Paint is light
On muscle that in humble radiance
Proclaims the heart of ritual, work and dance.

11. Bircher Muesli

You may easily make it yourself the night before,
When a light burns in the kitchen and you hear
The owl in the tree as though it were in your ear.
Take two cups of rolled oats, and then no more
Than one and three-quarters of rich milk (which you pour
Over the oats, together with a clear
Quarter of a cup of apple juice and near
As much of lemon). Close the cold door
Of the fridge, with the bowl inside, while you explore
Your dreams. Then in the morning commandeer
Thick yoghurt; honey; redcurrant's garnet sphere;
Apple, rasped finely (but discard the core).
Patients of Dr. Bircher-Benner grew
Frisky on this concoction. So can you.

12. Another view of the Zytglogge

At nightfall you can take a hundred paces
Out of the Goldener Schlüssel (strolling, not striding)
To the Zytglogge, where its many faces
Show you that time is merely the dividing
Of something that may or may not exist already
Before you measure it. It gives no reasons
Why you should find yourself the merest eddy
In its great river of the hours and seasons.

In fact, the whole apportionment is yours.
Its summonings and whirrings demonstrate
That you yourself are the substance and the cause
Of this malign dimension you create.
Though as its trumpet tootles, you can eat
Hot braziered chestnuts in the cobbled street.

13. Rudolf Buchbinder at the Kunst-Casino

A further few hundred paces takes you to
The Kultur-Casino, where music much less old
Than all those tootings makes its own to-do
In the great hall's decorous cream and gold,
And those who hear it are not passers-by
But have been drawn to its magnificence
Long in advance, knowing their francs can buy
The privileges of an audience.

A simple contract. Not so simple is
The way the power moves down the pianist's arms
Into his working hands. That power is his,
But all the descending chords belong to Brahms.
It's obvious that art is life perfected,
Yet see: how strangely Brahms is resurrected!

14. At the Nydeggbrücke

Here, where the Aare makes a hairpin of
The elevated city, lives a bear
In a bear pit, like a cellared Romanov,
Where people come in awe and shame to stare
Down at the barkless logs and sculpted boulders
For glimpses of something like a shambling rug,
One of those animals whose feet are shoulders
That pace the tedious earth, and sometimes hug.

By day its name is Finn, and out of pity
Is thrown the rationed scraps of its defeat.
But when night comes in the deserted city
It claims its heritage, and up the street
Parades in coloured flags, while from its head
Break tongues of fire on golden gingerbread.

In memory of John Bayley

Buxton and Bayley
And a junior Tolkien:
   The traveller's guides.

'Bayley' with a 'y'!
'Buxton' sounds like Lucky Jim!
   Expectations baulked.

His vision of me
As someone of character
   Without form and void.

My Shakespeare essay
At 6.00; thinking of meeting
   Ginsberg at 8.10!

What was it I wrote
That made him quite so thoughtful?
   Not worth the pausing.

He missed the Auden
Dinner through 'flu' but was up
   And about next day.

. . .

He knew what he knew
Without thinking about it,
   And spoke like a child.

Shrugging his shoulders
Forwards, wriggling with impish
  Delight, eyes gleaming.

The words coming out
Of his rounded lips like sauce
  From an old bottle.

After a chortle,
The sudden ruminative
  Wistfulness: 'Quite so.'

A gleam of hope, then
Sadness at idiocy:
  'You may well be right.'

. . .

He moved into the
Old Milner Rooms, painted them
  Blue. 'Looks good!' I said.

Tips from a tutor:
Very much cheaper to buy
  Suède shoes from Woolworth's.

Thinly-sliced kipper
Is as nice as smoked salmon
  And cheaper (half-true).

That poem of Keats
I had somehow passed over:
   'Charming is it not?'

Does my essay work?
Or doesn't it work? He gives
   Me an acid drop.

.   .   .

Coming up the stairs
With shopping bags, his bride of
   The previous year.

Iris, who like him
Was author of a novel.
   Who knew which would last?

Iris, flirtatious
With her probing tenor voice
   And ethical smock.

Iris, who once took
Great care to introduce me
   To my own father.

Bayley and Murdoch:
Famous comedy duo,
   Locked in devotion.

We cook for them Pope's
Knuckle of veal (for as long
   As the Dean's sermon).

Eating wild cresses
From their garden stream: would we
    Suffer liver flukes?

          .   .   .

    New College winter:
Pyjama bottoms peeping
    Below his trousers.

    Cranking with the car
In gear, he ran himself down:
    His leg was broken.

    Then within the year,
The car battery was dead:
    He did it again.

    The leg is mending,
A full kettle on his toe,
    Lifted and lowered.

    Delight at the cold:
'The owl for all his feathers . . .'
    Madeline asleep.

          .   .   .

    A dedication
To him from grateful Auden?
    The wrong John Bayley!

These poor random thoughts:
My too-late gratitude to
   The right John Bayley.

To read a poem
And know that it was for me,
   Because he said so.

Currents in the flood,
Confluence of molecules,
   A passing eddy.

Keeper of the Fire

In memory of Saul Touster (1925—2018)

1.

Among the googols of irrelevant facts today
Is the one I feared to find: a terminal date
To your career of distinction as poet and lawyer.

It is not only a shocking rent
In your personal fabric of space and time
But now a plain event in the public account

Occurring after the latest, and now the last
Of your fond communiqués of bravado,
Written 'from the edge of eternity.'

We had long exchanged these messages of affection
And wry good cheer, as though we had somehow given birth
To our own elderly selves, almost by accident.

Surprised at survival, dismayed at the vagaries
Of that weak organ of circulation and delay
Which turns hope or dismay into imperfect prayers.

2.

We met in Buffalo in 1962, an ivy-creepered campus
With a famed collection of manuscripts,
A temple in wild country.

And you, the young Saul, gentle doyen
Of its welcoming party, with your caressing speech
And your Harold Lloyd glasses, proclaiming

Rosenzweig's idea of the virtues of Judaism
As a fire in a clearing in a wilderness,
Shedding its light, but rooted to the spot.

Christians take torches from this fire,
Dashing into the darkness to bring its light
To the rest of the forest. But the light of these torches

Would expire unless relighted at the source.
This was your idea of a university:
Keeper of the fire, for torches to be rekindled there.

But I was no Christian, and I then knew nothing
Of my eighth share of your brethren's blood,
An ignorant child of a monstrous decade.

You were reasonably to cite Sheinson's Haggadah:
'How is it possible to speak of or to God in 1946?'
Having to deal with the monsters we ourselves had created.

Here, then, at the cradle of the hopeful 1960s,
The DP camps barely five years closed
And poems proclaiming at best the smallest decencies

While in the country of the Vile Antagonist
Your Catholic President was to declare himself,
As if already extinguished, a kind of donut.

And the young prepared simply to enjoy themselves
For ever and ever, as though that would dispel those shadows
Etched into evil, that could be printed off again.

3.

A snow-belt winter saw head-high ploughfuls
Packed where once we parked our battered De Soto,
The cistern freezing in our grey-and-green apartment

Where Prue cheered us with Gogol-Mogol
(Egg yolk and Demerara) while I marked papers
On the intentions of Nashe's *Unfortunate Traveller*

And Sophie practised walking, making her first friend
With serious Penny next door. We pulled her,
Rosy in her snow-suit and sled, through the approach

To Niagara where the ice stood a foot thick
On the spray side of the coppice of trees,
And they said we were crazy to take her out.

And our season of introductions was well advanced:
Turkey and apple pie with Mrs Abbott
And her ugly bull-dog, unnervingly called Sophia.

Party after party, housewarmings and readings,
You, Saul, as the prime chairman of good cheer
Along with Aaron, and Al, and the commanding Oscar.

Provider of punch and appeaser of the Pos,
Sculptor of verses of the still life,
Frozen moments aching for perfection.

You worked in a vein of passionate directness
In the admired manner of Americans (the latest was Lowell)
Whose lives were always alive, still but not dead

Leading the past to its perfection and regrets,
Like an apple and its amorous adventures,
Like an apple that might as well be a person.

You were yearning for the happiness that poetry
Tells us we may work to deserve
If we can understand the warnings within it.

Your Salo was a creation of the night,
Vagrant and dispossessed, with a grudge against time
And a nose for the winds and restlessness of the city.

4.

Spring melted in Allegany
Where we all took to the woods
In a green-boarded cabin dripping from its eaves

And the woodchucks and chipmunks
Scuttling in the brush
Muttered their farewells to winter.

Idle days of young families together,
Free of their students and the dark city,
A controlled experiment in creative living.

Tasha scribbling, Sophie testing
Her toes, and madcap Jonnie
Shy behind Helen's dirndl.

Prue managing the imperfect plumbing
With recourse to the stream below
For the dunking of dishes.

I quoted our favourite sage's
'And now she cleans her teeth into the lake'
As an unusual communion with nature

And it pleased your calculating mind
As another kind of legal fiction
To our rights *usque ad inferos.*

Beyond us, between the trees
The orange eyes of racoons
Watched our performances in wonder.

Parents in damp ponchos, vying
In badminton and *bouts rimés,*
Upright as bears in holiday attire

With steak on an open fire and yams
In the embers which you tendered
With recitations and a hopeful stick.

5.

Our year was soon gone, across
The continent and back to New York.
You took our trunks to Railway Express

And saw us off at the downtown docks
Where the ocean waited (who names the seas
Since no one lives on them?).

You lamented the passing of time
As what it can come to seem:
The lapse of affection in divergence.

And in all the following decades
What became of the feel and length of our lives
Which now appeared as descriptions and rumours?

Your marriages expired, like unrenewed
Permits for happiness. Your letters
Were sometimes thick with poems.

There was gossip from the poetic front:
Olsen the Queen Bee; the Pos, now married,
Beating up the twice-beat Corso.

Your parties went swimmingly,
'And those who couldn't swim
Just floated off.' And there was good advice:

'Clear away the debris . . . let your voice
Come upon you like an Indian from ambush,
At a casual turn in the path.'

Later, Brandeis and administration
Claimed your pacifying talents.
You worked on the great Holmes and the Civil War

And at Lowell's funeral were reminded not only of Shaw
And his Black regiment, but of poets
As unexceptional, their deaths as men.

You also met Irene in 1977, woman
'With Irenic qualities,' yours
For more than forty years.

6.

For whom, now, these words are intended,
Though anyone may read them, since
The private also has its public occasions.

Dear Saul, we should have seen more of you.
That time you were in London
And called, but we were in Wales!

In your eighties you leaped an Oxford gate
And pretended not to be bothered
By torn trousers: an English reaction.

You lamented with us the renewal of the monstrous,
The forgetting that is the prelude to ignorance,
The march on reason, the release of hatred.

And you wrote your own late poems of remembrance,
Reminding us that the stories we tell are the real truth
And that even judges should undertake a study of poetry.

And when we met you at that Dream Hotel
In the underwater blues of its mirrored lobby
You were still the enthusiast of life we had long known

And you expounded in the Met on Morandi
And his luminous *natura morta* with a gravity
That came of knowing how our lives

Are never still, but surely end up in stillness
And the fire that is the fire of knowledge
Is also the fire that will one day consume us.

Engagement Diaries

Old diaries have their uses: they remind you
That where you went, and who you met, and who
You hoped to meet, were never set in stone.
These things that happened once were just appointments,
And when the scribbled hopes were put behind you,
You turned the page and there was something new.
The days were filled, and you were not alone,
Despite the no-shows and the disappointments.

Look back upon the pages: they are prayers
To a god of daily life, brief pencilled mixtures
Of thrill or secrecy, routine or dread.
But what now moves you, catching you unawares,
Are not these social choices, but the fixtures:
Those sacred dates, the birthdays of the dead.

Photograph Albums

I once wrote of our chance lives and their meeting
As the joining of tributary streams, as though
A river, moving on to its unknown destination
Brought a determination in its mingled waters
Like a promise from an equally unknown source.

Where to? Where from? are questions the river itself
Can never answer at the moment of its passing.
Its swirling and gathering are compelled by confluence
Till its levels turn fields to a fine stubble
And cows stand on their nervous reflections.

So it is with these photographs slipped into
An album that pursues a name or a place
And leaves hanging the lines of adventure
(A removal to another continent, a marriage)
And the mysterious hiatuses within the dynasty.

Lives are interwoven, meeting and crossing
And passing, like a stuff that might roll on for ever,
Great heavy bolts of it, patterned with kinship
And the chosen colours of daily family life,
Until the sharp shears meet within it.

Completing one album and starting another
Joins blood and requires a back-story
That would probably go on repeating itself
With all those surprising things to look forward to:
The pages that began with a baby end with a mother.

Four generations back, when the photographs begin,
The jaw or the stare, or the certain line of the hair,
Confirm the identity of those who knew they would be
Strangers to us, whose ghosts they saw glimmering
In the attentive eyes of the photographer.

Future observers seemed as theoretical and unlikely
As the columns and pastoral backdrops of the studio,
Hardly an expected consequence of the expensive occasion
Which stopped time dead in its polished chamber
With attendant flowers, like a funeral.

But they guessed they were time-travellers, and adjusted
Their expressions accordingly with a serene self-assurance.
Or that blanker look which disguised their fear of failure
With mistrust of the world which chose to observe them.
There they are, offerings of a kind. Frail heroes of light.

Before we Met—and After

for Prue at 80

1. Making for the Buoy

The yellow buoy is only what it is,
A yellow plastic sphere, unmoving and apart,
A boundary, an empty exclamation
Sedate upon the water, a tethered moon.
Beyond are only boats, and the open sea.

To touch it, and return, is everything.
Just for this moment you have set your heart
On reaching, through this liquid element,
The point at which achievement says to you
That nothing is therefore unattainable.

Your hands move upon the dappled surface and part
The gelatine skeins as if to open them
And see below you all you must pass over:
Stirred sand like a snow-globe, waving weed,
And the one trailing chain that marks your goal.

You harbour these desires throughout your life,
Exemplary of gesture as of will,
Something for which you're ready to make a start
By striking out, smoothly, with firm strokes,
Raising your head for breath, and lowering it

Into the cool still water, your eyes fixed
On nothing but that inward concentration
Of motion and purpose that you have possessed
Ever since your mother threw you into life,
And, wanting you to swim, into the Dart.

2. Pony

The serene child, left to her own devices,
Has chosen to become a helmeted centaur.

As her nose and chin advance through the air,
Her fair hair follows, like a pavane.

Her everywhere is the map in her head
Of a country without boundaries.

There may be some clip-clop on a stretch of road
Or a standing in the river, gently snorting.

But all the hinterland is bramble fields
And a holly path beside the woods

Where the divots stand in the tan earth
Proud as biscuits, as she rides on

To secret woods within the woods
Where the floor is an indetermination of needles,

Where the buzzards whoop above the tree tops
And ghastly fungi bulge like wounds.

It is safe to say that elegant ambulation
May be an end in itself, an adventure.

Where he goes, she goes;
Where she goes, he goes.

The arrangement is completely satisfying,
Like some sort of agreed marriage

In which a singleness of purpose
Finds its mysterious reciprocation.

3. Britten at Dartington

How you loved his folk-songs, and most of all 'The Foggy, Foggy Dew',
With its jaunty joke about the weaver's bastard.
But it wasn't that so much as the open feminine yearning
That spoke to you then, even as a child,
The child of your mother, who could not begin to think
Of the time to come when you would become a mother yourself.

Frizzy-haired Ben, blinking post-flu in the Yarner sun
In pyjamas, jersey, and dormitory braided dressing-gown,
Had already learned how to communicate the wisdom
Of his persecuted gender and at the very same time
Appeal to be mothered, or to be a mother,
And an eleven-year-old child was for him a relic of the divine.

He showed you that the 'whip' was merely two hing-
-ed blocks of wood, and not a thong for horses.
Imo made one for you ('UM cha cha . . . UM cha cha')
Sending St Nicolas diving into his bath tub to cry:
'God be glorified!' And he played you bits of *Billy*
On the Yarner piano, and you called your goose Billy, too.

You found Ben a more obvious ally than the distant Peter,
Who had played God with a lampshade over his head,
And whose fascinating voice, like a thin keening,
Arrived as though from a very great distance over
Snowy summits and sunsets and pastoral meadows
With a sense of passing, like the whole of folklore.

But you loved the both of them for loving your mother,
And you knew even at that innocent age
The true love that needs no exaggeration
When you raised smiles by calling for that risqué encore:
'So I hauled her into bed and I covered up her head
Just to keep her from the foggy, foggy dew.'

4. Fieldfare

You brought a fieldfare in from the coldest winter
That you (or anyone) had ever known.
You saw a glint in one of its eyes like a splinter
Of light leaking out to search for a sky
That had shut to it for ever, still as a stone.
You held it close, and did not want it to die.

But like many of our fears this had happened already.
Its soft body in its stiff feathers felt warm.
You could imagine its fast heart beating steady
In anxiety, as though preparing to fly.
You held it even closer, to keep it from harm.
If it was warm, how could it ever die?

So cold outside, so cold! It was still snowing.
Your lashes blurred your eyes with flecks of snow
So that you could hardly see where you were going.
Fingers were frozen from snowballs you scooped up
So you could barely feel them move, although
They cradled the limp fieldfare like a cup.

No wonder it felt warm and seemed to be living.
Your mother knew better, and said it had to be out
Of the house by bed-time. Nature is unforgiving,
And mothers, too. For death does not keep its peace.
It is not merely stillness, and without a doubt
It is a terrible process that will never cease.

5. The Jancy

In peace time the Channel is open
To the lights of buoys floating
Like nests past you in the *Jancy*,—
Neither Jack nor Nancy,
Jaunty androgynous name for a boat.

Taking the wheel at night,
A duty of work
And the privilege of playing
At a journey once made
Across an ocean where U-Boats lurked.

Your hair bleached by the sun,
Salty eyebrows, and knees
Brown beneath your shorts:
The whole of life in your fingers,
The others dreaming through possibilities.

The boards tremble to the motor
As your hands tremble at the chance
Of turning the wheel towards
Adventure, your sleepless eyes
Searching in vain for the coast of France.

6. 'Levavi Oculos'

School didn't suit you, since
You'd been ten years without it.
And furthermore
Why weren't you allowed to keep
Your mice in your drawer?

That lingering aroma
Of over-boiled cabbage,
The wooden panels,
The interference with freedoms,
And frozen flannels.

School, you soon decided,
Was simply for running away from.
In sensible frustration
You promptly marched away
As far as the station.

Whatever contingent truths
You learned at school, for you
One was transcendent:
To be yourself, you must
Be independent.

Resistance in proceeding
Was the lesson to be learned
In reaching the heights,
Just as to make them fly,
You tug at kites.

7. Staying with the Wedgwoods

Two of them, two Ralphs, friends indeed and dear second cousins:
Yours the unlikely eponym of a steam locomotive
Puffing its way from London northwards, the 'Sir Ralph Wedgwood',
Named for the boss of the London Northern and Eastern Railway;
His the eccentric grand old man of British music,
Giving his puzzled fans a concerto for (Good Lord!) the tuba.
Both of them flattering avatars strangely alike, producing
Wonderful sounds from pistons, and an ample amount of moisture.
Could it, that engine, have carried me back with my parents,
Back from the digs and glens of wind-swept Aberdeenshire,
While it was still in service, prior to '42,
When in the Baedeker Raid on the York North Shed it exploded?
You were more likely, however, to travel to London from Devon,
Giving our journeying maps no reason for overlapping.
Later the 'fifties found us in all-unknowing apartness,
I for some weeks perhaps on the windy shores of the Var,
You, in your convalescence from shingles, alone with the Wedgwoods,
Parents of one of your mother's Sapphic companions from Oxford,
Generous fostering just like a quasi-Trollopean sojourn
Cunningly brought about to forestall an unsuitable meeting.
(I myself, I suppose, in an earlier hide-bound period
Might have been felt to be not-quite-right, as was your father,
Drawn as he was from a rural and clerical background,
Wooing the orphaned niece of a grand political name).
Ralph was so kind to you, and Lady Wedgwood also,
Giving you when you left a calf-bound set of Jane Austens
(Second and first editions, as you never seemed to notice,
Carrying them all around for years in your bicycle basket).
Mistress of rectitude, Jane, prompt to detect our failings,

Beacon of wit and truth for a lonely girl in her teens.
Odious word 'teenager', at that time barely invented,
Signalling purchasing power of proletarian jeans
(Only our parents' choices for us, the grey flannel trousers
Everyone wore, the ties, the jerseys and sensible skirts).
Would I had known you then! Perhaps I would have come calling
Out of the blue, with a grin, and breaching convention,
Faithful as Frank Tregear dismaying poor Lady Cantrip,
Finding you there with the Wedgwoods, sitting before the fire,
Talking of nothing much while turning a glass in your fingers,
Gossiping after dinner and cupping the glass in your hands,
Thinking perhaps of me, while warming the old man's brandy.

8. At the Gallery

You said your farewell to Corky. There was no place
For a pony in 1950s Islington,
Though somewhere in the busy heart were memories
Of what he felt like: the pace, the elevation,
Heels bobbing against the moving flanks.
No wonder that your favourite painting, on visits
To the Gallery on those private Sunday mornings,
Was *Charles I on Horseback*, the king so wistful
With his sad red eyes and hopeful smile,
The horse, with its tiny head tucked in, immense
In exploit, distinguished in muscled breast and girth.

9. Vitelloni

Self-protective in the rumbling train to Florence,
    Nervous and angry at
Too-attentive *vitelloni*, in abhorrence
    'Noli me tangere'
You with great resourcefulness proclaimed.

No-one ever could imagine you as starry-
    Eyed—the equestrian,
Sailor, rebel, linguist, nanny *alla pari*,
    Shaming testosterone,
Frowning at them, taming the untamed.

10. Interviews

Ever the staunchest of boarding-school rebels,
You were totally traumatized by gaunt Girton
With its meant-to-be-helpful wardrobe labels
And their taxonomy of clean underwear,
Example of that Cantabridgean high-mindedness
That tuned its verses 'a wee bit sharp'
As though a poem could be made to convince
Like a fifth in the upper reaches of a harp,
And rise above the dismal flatness
Of the landscape, and its miasmal air.

Shocking to think of your going there
And not to Oxford (with its walkable hills
Where the poets perceive the buried life
With a wry ruefulness, and do not let
Their minds get much above themselves).
Doubtless you never would have failed
To select the bust-bodice of the week,
Eager as a nun unveiled,
But what of Katie Lea? And me?
My God, we never would have met!

11. The Unities

Once seen, you were unaccountably in my head,
Cycling superbly and tangentially across my life
In your paisley dress of fine cotton with its pattern
Of looping azure, salmon, and the palest teal.

I looked for you at lectures, looked sideways
Towards your blonde hair and your alert and lifted chin.
What was it that Trypanis was saying about universals?
'*Katholou*', he intoned, looking up at the ceiling of Schools.

I thought *To Kalon* the likeliest of these universals
And best deserved of that dubious family of *Katholou*
And that here was its defiant embodiment
Not to be sought in either ceilings or theory.

Francis brought us together in the same room at the same time,
Like a piece of illusionist's theatre, and he, the impresario,
Became also the unwilling and disbelieving audience,
Knowing and yet not knowing how the trick was done.

12. Absence

The Freshers' Photo of '57
Reveals you as typically not there.
All the others (some in earrings!)
Make the duty seem tedious
In each averted blush or stare.

And I remember how already
You were agonizingly adept
At the behaviour that beauty
Soon discovers, those appointments
Unnecessary to accept.

Yes, you were very much invited.
Inevitably the cards thickened
Upon your mantelpiece, and hosts
Made unconvincing promises
As the general expectation quickened.

Heads turned towards the spaces
That you had lately left. Elsewhere
Could suddenly seem desirable
As note after note littered the desk
Beside your empty library chair.

Easy to feel that I too had claims
On you. Suspense: I called
For you at LMH, then had
To sit next door and chat to Dee,
Polite, with coffee, unenthralled.

But soon enough, it seemed to me,
You took to my company,—whether
Across those squelchy Marston fields,
Out at the Scala, or a curry,—
And we could then be absent together.

13. Reading Room

I could babble on till baboons inhabit Babylon—C. P. M.

The notes were scribbled on
Those yellow slips for filling
The spaces left by volumes
We'd taken from the shelves.

Small snapshots of protest,
Boredom, or inquiry
That in those afternoon hours
Seemed to write themselves.

'Where on earth have you gone?'
'I want to talk to you
Sometime—remind me.'
'I will see you in the Taj.'

Much more fascinating
Than the level lines of lyrics,
Weightier than the speech
Of archangels and monsters.

The words of life itself
Sketching its stumbling path
Through the warm fingers
And their stub of blunt pencil.

14. Intruder

That room in which you ceased to be a child,
A Georgian attic, papered to the ceiling
With encouraging flowers and haunted by the wraiths
Of all the housemaids that had ever slept there,
Felt far from the safety of your Devon farm.
A parapet that ran along the terrace
Seemed likely to give access to intruders
To be repelled by the ancient fencing foil
You kept at hand beneath your eiderdown.
And there I sat myself, admitted both
To your loving person and your body
Moving at ease among its surfaces,
Moving in natural grace of limb and skin,
Bending for shoes or reaching for a book,
Belonging to all that was familiar,
Belonging both to you and to your chosen future.
And I had come in that hope of being chosen,
Ready to choose myself, thinking that to choose
Was nothing like a bold appropriation
That maids have always feared, and then desired,
To be parried like the feeble thrust of steel,
But more the claiming of a mysterious right,
Long known, but half-forgotten, half-remembered,
That the strong beating of the blood, flooding
Upon me, in confusion, told me of.

15. *Waverley, 4.05*

At Waverley, at Waverley,
Although I didn't show it,
I knew a certain thing that
Needed knowing,
At Waverley.

A resolve in the heart
Deeper than any words,
An unexpected reward
After some time apart,
At Waverley.

Beneath that iron edifice
And its dulled reverberation of voices
Your lips reached up to mine
With a fresh Scottish kiss,
At Waverley, at Waverley.

I had come to stay with your sister
In Scott's metropolis,
And you were just like yourself
When you met me with a kiss
At Waverley, at Waverley.

Greeting you there, after empty weeks at home
When your existence seemed a fabulous rumour,
I was restored to a possession of myself
Of which you were an indissoluble part.

I had thought that my life would never begin.
But there you were, and no thought of an ending,
Like a landscape bathed in light, where legends start,
Like a won position at chess, that needs no defending.

You put your arm in mine at Waverley
And I was willingly led out of the concourse
Into our resumed and now entirely certain life
Whose truth possessed me with a renewed force
At Waverley, at Waverley.

The name was strange—Waverley,
So appropriate for a railway station
With its moods of hesitation and goodbye,
But inappropriate for me

When for once, and at once, and for all time,
With a kiss that was both a reminder and a promise,
A perfect fresh kiss that could never lie,
I knew that I would never say goodbye.

16. 29a

Our first tenancy as new recruits
To the wedded life—£5 a week,
A kindness from my feckless moral tutor.

The top floor of his house, shared with au pairs,
Mullioned windows under the eaves,
The bed in the bathroom, with a blue-flamed geyser.

We were happy in such an ad hoc establishment.
He never asked for the rent. We lived
In style, though using the tradesmen's entrance.

We looked out over a suburban hinterland
Of garden and orchard and Raymond's donkey.
Sophie's cot was on the landing.

Other members of his menagerie took
To assailing us. The porcupine ate her cereal.
The monkey at his dinners leaped from the bookcase.

Rats chewed the fingers of his sons,
While the porcupine wandered into LMH
And fell from a balcony that was sadly unsafe.

Guests left their coats on top of Sophie's cot
To eat our *civet de lièvre*
And Lancashire cheese with a corner-shop bottle.

Such for a time was our heady universe,
And you were the decisive centre
Of life that is always to be lived without rehearsal.

17. Daughters

Taking breath, like diving for pearls.
Your body wet and flowering, like bursting from the sea.
Whatever our daughters got up to inside you,

Whatever their submarine intuitions, we shall never know.
Birth was the big secret, the long-saved surprise,
The decisive three acts, like a brilliant play.

There was also the continuation of our negotiations,
A watchfulness and admiration of unique personalities.
What comes first to mind?

Sophie on the back-seat webbing of 482-EE
With an icebox of cold jewels against the Painted Desert
Which hit us unexpectedly one morning with 113°.

Louisa in the air, laughing as if for ever,
Chubby but weightless, before falling
Back into my raised arms.

Emily bent over with her head in the foam
Looking at us between her legs, to locate and invert
Our pursuing presence, like wolves in Neverland.

And that past is still what it was, though no longer the present,
When all their long futures had their own ideas, too,
Of making their appointed entrances.

Afresh

The flowers are freshly worked: bluebells,
Magenta curls like machined steel
Dripping from damp stalks; excited
Explosions of thrift, searching for sun.

The thrift is opposing the blue with pink
As it did last season, and the season before,
And the bluebells are opposing the green with blue
As they will go on doing in the future.

Isn't it an illusion, beginning all over?
An illusion born of flowers performing
Afresh their grey-cornered text
In the empty theatre of the world?

For you and me such roles are forbidden.
All we can do is carry on where we left off,
Like these pebbles whose shapes as they dwindle
Are models of what they have long been.

Our own text is nearly finished. We carry it
Possessively, knowing there is only one version.
It is like a loan, for which we must be grateful,
The flyleaf stamped, but no chance of renewal.

Garden

The old rose celebrates its jubilee,
Scaling the lilac, glimmering in the dawn.
Who knew that fifty years would see it last
    Another summer in the light?
We've cradled all the badges it has worn,
    Its apricot dissolved to white,
Clustered in bowls of water on the table.

And soon, the arms of ancient fruit trees, full
Of their plump astounding progeny,
Also bend down before the dwindling year
    And we shall find it not too late
To look up in the evening to see
    Those well-remembered shapes and weight
And gather them in bowls upon the table.

The soil has welcomed everything it can.
The branches lighten, and the twigs are bare.
The sun is weary of performing, smiles
    A little, takes an early bow.
For all we know, the earth has secrets there
    Where the damp leaves gather, but for now
The bowl is empty on the winter table.

Hallowe'en

The long summer, with its butterflies and pale grasses
Has stiffened in the calendar. The busy woodpecker
Is no longer rattling in her cupboard, and the stream,
Once dry, now seethes in its tiered descent
To the primordial waters that it longs for,
Waiting beyond the wood and the valley fields.

Such is the gravity and the withdrawal
That brings us to our origins and to our dead.
Who are they, those who once were merely living
And before that, nowhere? What place do they assume,
And where? Who do they think they are? Who?
What makes you think they come when they are called?

Now all the butterflies have gone where they go to
And the appropriate bird in the autumn tree
Is the baleful owl, interrogating the saints
(Who? Who?), and the clocks release their hour,
That bubble in the drip of time that makes
It flow more freely and the patient sleep.

The year is turning over as the sea does
With the slightest of sighs. A sheet stirs on the floor.
At this, we can only drink to the sanctity of the moment.
The glasses are filled. The memories cohere
As shapes in a darkening room. The toast is to
Those who we loved but who cannot drink with us.

Shadows

Evening comes quickly now, but the room at night
Is never completely dark. Objects appear
To dissolve into an underwater grey
(The sightless mirror, the sweater on the chair
Glowing from the standby TV's goblin eye,
The crouching stool, the breathing chest of drawers)
Like animals that murmur, feed and sleep
And barely move all the night long in deep
Darkness, when the outdoors feels indoors.
What is it we're afraid of? The day will die
As we do. What if there are shadows there
Hiding some things that will not go away?
The curtain pales, so there is nothing to fear,
For yes, the shadows exist, but then there is light.

Old Trees

Here and there, in the civilities
Of urban gardens, you will sometimes find,
Beyond the furnished terraces, old trees
Crouching stiffly, as though their purposes
And histories had never been known at all.
They seem in endless winter, left behind
To interrupt a lawn or prop a wall.

They are like (but like is what the poet says,
Hardly to be believed beyond the page)
Our frozen selves, which lost their only gift
Of blossoming,— that time of light and lift
Of leaf before the consciousness of age,—
And once were orchards, their new branches thick
With fruit that glowed, and low enough to pick.

The Pool

That leap of youth, forever above a pool
That takes its time to receive the arms and legs:
It is a calculated recklessness,
A suspendedness half star and half grimace,
Intending a wild pose, rather than a means
Of deliberately entering the water.

Take courage from this extreme and vigorous art
Which thinks nothing of minor practicalities
Such as when and how some wise retreat is practical
Or even if that splash was possibly once your own,
As you approach, with cautiously lowered foot,
Colder and colder, the Roman steps of age.

X-ray

All that winter it was the sun that we missed,
With its lovely pulse that scatters the air to blue.
It was the winter when you surprisingly fell
(A closing gate, and running to get through).

You fell with a headlong tumble and a twist,
And amongst all the attention and discomfort
I was reminded of the daily miracle
That blood continues to move in our veins at all.

The clouds come low over the pass like animals,
At a steady pace, timid but determined.
No hill can block them, dispersed as mist,
Nor trees, nor gates broken and never mended.

We wake, and our bodies are obligingly there
Like the first sunrise or a triumph of conjuring.
We piece together whatever future we have
Day by day, as a familiar pastime.

Should we suppose the sun not there when we fail
To see it, like the lost piece of a puzzle?
If anything is missing, we should not blame it,
Or expect it. Things have a habit of turning up.

So beneath our dailiness the cycle goes on,
And the dead leaf retains its skeleton,
And one day certainly, perhaps on a Tuesday,
The sunshine will return as though never away.

Now when you move your hand over the pieces
Or towards me over the table, I see only
That miracle and the many tiny bones,
The pure grace of it, and the ghost of the wrist.

Too Late

I dreamed I lay asleep beside you.
It was too late to touch you, or call out.

The bees were pulling at the roses, and
Some cloud stuff stretching in the summer air.

My mind was capable of thoughts.
My position had a familiar feel.

My mind knew what it was about.
My shape knew nothing but itself.

I longed to wake and find you, but
I could not move. I could not stir my hand.

My body was a ghost of sorts,
Knowing where it was. It was elsewhere,

Some bird or other gave a shout,
Intending to call the day to order.

But nothing was happening, and nothing more,
It seemed, was ever going to happen.

I could not stir my hand to let you know
That I was there. I could not stir.

Just for that moment there was no future,
No hope at all of going back.

No memory of whatever brought me there,
Though I knew it was my entire life.

I longed to turn and see you,
To let you know I hadn't gone away.

But all the weight of me was in the chair
Where I was fast asleep. You were not there.

Breath

The fire is dead. No glow.
Grey, with no memory
Of burning. All is sunk low,
The log a black crust of tree.

But open the vent, a twist
Of brass at the front of the stove.
Just two half-turns of the wrist
And the fire is again alive.

Like a patient with oxygen,
Or a morning dreamer where
Turning lets lungs deepen
To the morning's gift of air.

So with the heart's firing,
Gulping its precious ichor:
Slowing right down, the wiring
Falters. Then it beats quicker.

It is life's thread unwound,
As it will, from its frail spindles,
Then catching, like the sound
Of a breath as the flame rekindles.

Somewhere

Somewhere I once belonged,
Who knows where?
But like the map englobed
My journey's clear.
I must find out.
I must go there.
For the past is space
That must be crossed,
Memory a face
That's not quite lost.

Somewhere within me
A remembered promise,
Hard to misprove,
A spoken word
That is love's premise,
Trajectory of bird
When it migrates
In secret purpose,
However hard
The route proposed.

Let the exile then return
In evening peace
However late,
As though from sleep
And in forgiveness,
With homecoming's pace
And horizon's red
Where clouds hovered,
And somewhere overhead
The uncorking sound of geese.

The Ferryman

I didn't know if I was asleep or awake.
'Ferryman,' I called out. 'Are you there?'
For it was barely light enough to prove
His presence there at all. The water lapped
Against his boat, pole sucking at the mud.
      I listened to my blood.

I didn't know if it was early or late.
'Ferryman,' I called out. 'Are you waiting?'
I wasn't ready. Again, I couldn't move.
'Early, is it? Or late?' The birds were crying
As if to greet, or to lament, the day.
      The ferryman said: 'It's late.'

No Turning

Time is telling tales behind my back,
   That I might stay to hear
   (I would be none the wiser).

To reach the bottom of the present page!
   Another hill to climb
   With all the rage of youth!

There is no turning from the track.
   The mountainside is sheer.
   The moon's a miser.

The one lit window that I hope to see
   May well be shuttered now.
   The mysteries endure.

Perhaps I shall become that surprised sage
   Who woke for the last time
   Knowing, for once, the truth.

Three words only ('You and me')
   Define the when and how.
   And that's enough, for sure.

Acknowledgements and Notes

Acknowledgements are made to the following magazines, pamphlets and web-sites, in which some of these poems first appeared: *Agenda, Not Altogether Ripe,* the *Oxford Magazine, Oxford Poetry, Oxford Review of Books, Poetry Nation Review, Slim Pickings, Spectator, Standpoint, The Critic, The Florio Society, Times Literary Supplement* and *Wild Court.*

'Fulehung' was commissioned by the painter Joost de Jonge, as a response to one of his paintings, and as part of his ekphrastic project, *De Gids.* The Fulehung is a masked jester who runs in the streets of Thun on the last Monday in September, frightening children and giving treats to them. 'The Giant' is about Mount Etna. 'Siege' was written in response to a request from the composer Nicola LeFanu for a text for a large-scale work for soprano and orchestra: a version of it was set as 'The Crimson Bird' and first performed by Rachel Nicholls and the BBC Symphony Orchestra conducted by Ilan Volkov on 17 February 2017 at the Barbican Centre. The final prayer may be translated as: 'He who makes peace in high places, He will make peace for us and for all Israel, and let us say Amen.' 'A Week in Bern' was published as a pamphlet by the Clutag Press in 2016.